I0016797

Windows 3.1

Alan Chelak

Image 34 # 1

Image 34 Poetry Series

©2014 Alan Chelak
ISBN-13: 978-1-312-70705-4
All Rights Granted. Any part of this
book maybe reproduced in any form
or by an electronic or mechanical
means, including information storage
and retrieval systems, without
permission in writing from the
publisher.

God just retweeted a tweet.
Including the very poor,
who are of interest to the
story line in brief. – X –

A women, bent out of shape,
trying   to   sell   car
insurance. A clock ticking
with green hands. A red

man in the corner, cut in
half by pictures of me.
Pictures of me everywhere.
Then the letter from the

woman   at   the   Friends
School,   looking   for   an
escape on October 9th for
her sweet little children –

– take them to the porn
section?   Porn   section:
SEND   News   in: Thomas
Pynchon, mute horn, new

movie. Clicks to links to
clicks   to   world

notifications, a forgotten
birthday party, a forgotten

weed dating event (mill
creek farms), a new
acceptance letter, that guy
who wanted to sleep with

Pablo has an event called
last Christmas, Melanie
likes the Candy Game,
Daragh mentioned me in a

comment, Meghan's lost some
weight, pre-ordered watches
are 70% off retail, Aunt
Mary is drunk on cat-moon

videos, Duncan is so happy
he doesn't have to see any
of us anymore, Colin wants
people to text him at work,

Meghan has a new pair of
glasses(!), Tyree may or
may not have had a baby,
Amanda cannot make pancakes

"normal", Gabriel is with
some woman by a fridge and
people like it (34), Mary
has something to say about

her husband being like her
children via image of
little girl holding flower
behind her back, kissing

little boy whose hat comes
off his head, Danny Vo also
appears to have had a
child, I should stop riding

mass transit and just get
car insurance already, Jeff
continues to post about his
deeply held political

convictions, Meghan really
likes her friend Rachel
Babble, Alissa hand dyed
her koma shirt pink (like),

Philly AIDS Thrift has an
urgent message re: their

block   party   tomorrow
afternoon, a man or perhaps

a woman with his or her
tongue out stands in front
of a weather forcast, Brian
has a movie suggestion (it

made him cry) -- Carol
agrees with this suggestion
(the movie also made her
cry ;( ), Joseph O'Kennedy

is really into Mohammed
Ali's Daughter right now,
Coult has an opinion on
Derke Jeter, Jennifer says

hail satin -- our soft and
silky lord, Charissa says
her hair cut was indeed
good luck just as the

horoscope said it would be,
the bloody marry liberation
party has been suggested to
me, Cameron's mom got a

smart phone and she is
funny (according to
Cameron), Jennifer Renee
Eberle and Paul Henry

Eberle Got Married, Danny
Vo bought an ice coffee (25
people liked this), Joseph
O'Kennedy appears to be a

racist (7 people liked
this), Jenny Martin has a
dog video she'd like to
share, Paul Lamb hates the

Cops (nobody liked this),
Charissa Morningstar has
problems with her
fingernails?, Ren Liam has

an opinion about the sexual
habits of Human beings,
Ciara has an opinion about
drivers on the road, Jera

Sky likes Uber and Uber
will let me earn up to

$20/hour and $60k/year in fares driving in the Philly

suburbs with uberX! Joseph Marie Wilkinson spent the last couple of evenings thinking of what an amazing

time it is in small press publishing (61 people liked this).   Meghan has an optical illusion (trippy)

which two people liked -- it makes her think of Neil Patrick   Harris?   -- Meanwhile, Ged Ruggles

wants me to carry his book (available on Amazon), dead link asks if I'm looking for something -- we're

sorry the web address you entered   is   not   a functioning page on our site -- TRASH CAN -- Flower

of Iowa wants to do a
reading -- STAR // FOR
LATER -- Rick Gallagher NYT
Bestseller List-GNOV --

TRASHCAN -- Ralph Rodriguez
Philly Fun Guide -- Arcadia
in flames? Arcadia, green
text mapped background in

flames? PafA -- Tom
Stoppard's masterpiece is
one of the greatest plays
of the last 20 years -- a

tale of two centuries,
shifting as seamlessly
between eras as it does
between farcical comedy and

heartbreaking romance -- X
-- Session Timeout -- White
Exclamation Mark in Blue
Circle -- Red Ok -- Ok -- X

-- dump.fm -- horse in
rainbow background throds -

- and we've blocked it and
called your dad (surrounded

by trees) -- 19 squad in
the building -- september
october november december
january febuary -- any

latin guys hung guys big
shooters need deep
throating m4m -- <3 -- what
ever happened to @put?? --

Japanese symbols -- a
teenager drinks out of a
large green cup -- omg -- I
am a white jock 6'1" 200

lbs clean shaven, brown
hair, mostly smooth defined
beefy muscular body type.
Reply with full stats and -

- strawberry milky is back
-- omgomgomg<3 -- wut -- i
love it -- yayy -- kinny <3
-- im so happy -- me2 -- i

doubt he'll be coming back
here, he's focused on
trying not to starve to
death in Canada, I guess. -

- need some jams -- bright,
stop pretending u dont love
me -- so bright is ryder?
<3 -- omg he's Canadaian

too? -- janet jackson music
video -- ask the bar -- I'm
a NSA, no recip, non size
q, excellent oral provider.

-- oldbooth -- why you're
at a bar while chatting --
cmere<3 -- its a show.
I'll ask the promoter --

everyone knows ryder is in
love with me? -- i cant
upload a giant gif to ello
:\ -- is that even true? --

LINK -- 2 new dumps -- X --
purple trees -- barnes-
hut|N-Body   Building:

Barnes-Hut is a commonly

used tree algorithm that
represents a vast
improvement over direct
summation methods in

context of N-body
computation. -- VISIT PAGE
-- N-Body Building, Working
Out MPI Parallelization on

Barnes-Hut Oct-Tree --
Barnes-Hut -- Barnes-Hut --
What is a Barnes -- What is
a Barnes-Hut Oct-Tree? -- X

-- Verizon Email Login -- X
-- What does Amante Mean in
English? -- X -- Syllabus
for ENGL 251 2014 -- X --

Portal:Current Events
Wik... -- X -- Ellen
Moody's 'Net Writings an...
-- X -- gaskell the grey

woman -- X --

Gaskell|Gothic   Lit   &
Writi...   --   X   --   Simone
Zelitch | Writer, Te... - X

-- Lovely (Yumemiru Lovely
Boy) -- Girl with Pikachu -
- News: How the US Shrank
One Square Mile // Cowboys

by an american flag --
Search   for   Fugitive
Survivalist   Leads   to
'Haunted' Hotel // men in

the   woods   --   Amazon
Jungel's Nutrient Sorce:
Dead   African   Fish   //
rotting wood -- Ebola Death

Toll Passes 3k // people
building   houses   --
Obituary: Man 'Dispised'
the Kardashians // some

woman   --   Police: Footage
Shows Ghost at the Station
// fog on camera -- Dow
Rebounds, Rises 167 // bald

guy writing something down
-- Water on Earth Older
Than Sun, Earth itself //
children playing in ocean

-- POPUP -- X -- Sistine
Chapel   Getting   Better
Lights   //   human   body
exposed on ceiling -- Eric

Holder: Why He's Great, Why
He's Awful // Eric Holder
looks composed -- Britain
Joins US Coalition Against

ISIS // man in suit -- 35K
Pounds of Raw Chicken Found
Rotting in Truck // gross
water dripping from truck

//   Driver   allegedly
demanded ransom -- POLICE
LINE DO NOT CROSS // Okla.
Woman   Beheaded   by   Co-

Worker: Cops   --
'Intentional' Fire at FAA

Facility Grounds Planes //
Woman dropping her baby --

Ford Recalls 850K cars on
Short-Circuit Concerns //
pictures of cars in a lot -
- Megachurch Pastor May Sue

Rappers // a man screams
into a microphone -- Even
With Few Tunes, Jimi
Hendrix Biopic works //

Jimi plays guitar --
Hackers Exploit Security
Flaw Bigger Than Heartbleed
// man types on computer --

Sean Connery knockoff //
'Most Interesting Man' Now
a Landmine Hunter -- IZOD
now at KOHL'S // people in

clothing look happy // SHOP
NOW // buff man -- Swiss
Woman Treks 10K Miles Over
3 Years // woman in

sleeping bag in tent -- 5
Craziest Crimes of the Week
(!) // Blue Cat Litter Box
With Blue Scoop -- Here's

How Much America's Heaviest
Drinkers Drink // Cocktails
-- Two Cows Butting Heads
// Cows Really Don't Like

Cowbells, Study Finds --
Short Asian Man // Kim Jong
Un Has Disappeared -- Dark
circle with white line

(mouth) curving upwards //
Here's Your New Facebook
Alternative -- X -- Zavat-
e Gharb is a village in

Kelarestaq-e Sharqi Rural
District, in the Central
District of Chalus County,
Mazandaran Province, Iran.

At the 2006 census, its
population was 273, in 68
families. -- tumblr.com --

login -- kid a -- a fat man

without a shirt is talking
to a bald man with a shirt.
yellow text: NO WAYS MR.
LAHEY.   I   NEED   A

CHEEEBURGER. --   adam west
batman   //   antinwo   --
Argentina uses drones to
root   out   wealthy   tax

evaders // a store on the
corner of a street -- att
texting & driving, it i can
wai-- adamwest batman //

antinwo   recycled   vomit-
queen -- a diagram of a
tortiose -- men and women
at various stages in life

disecting a tortoise or
taking pictures of the
disection -- a man with a
beard   holding   the

tortoise's   head   in   his

hands, another man stands
in awe of the scene -- a
man and a women are

reconstructing the tortoise
from the disection, with a
longer neck for some reason
(perhaps) --   the man who

held the head before is now
working   on   this
reconstruction -- the fully
completed reconstruction of

the tortoise is now under
glass, presumably in a
museum -- amnhnyc: more
than 20,000 species of

plants and animals around
the   world   are   currently
under threat of extinction,
and hundreds vanish each

year. we don't always know
the   extact   time   of
extinction, but for the
Pinta   Island   giant

tortoise, the date was June
24th, 2012. -- On that day,
Lonesome George -- the
Galapagose Island tortoise

[Link] now on display at
the American Museum of
Natural History [Link], and
the last known member of

his species -- died of
natural causes. With him,
his species, Chelonoidis
abingdoni, vanished. Over

the last two years,
Wildlife Perservations
taxidermy experts have
worked closely with the

Museum scientists to
preserve Lonesome George as
he appeared in life -- down
to a missing toenail on his

left front foot. -- [Link]
Watch a video about the

preservation process, and learn much more about

Lonesome George. [Link] -- jeopardy-questions -- "BIG" DEAL -- IN THIS SWEET MOUNTAIN OF SONG, HOBOS

WILL FIND "A LAND THAT'S FAIR AND BRIGHT" -- This question originally aired on March 14th, 2005 --

Answer: The Big Rock Candy Mountain - X -- Frank Phillips (oil industrialist) -- born in

Scotia, Nebraska, -- Chris Hates Writing -- Social Media -- As a teen, I enjoyed sending handmade

cards to faraway friends. I spent hours meticulously cutting and glueing together pieces of card

stock, usually without the
faintest idea of what to
make or write, until I
produced something to my

liking. I let my hands do
the thinking. When I
graduated from high school
and went off to college, so

did I from cardmaking. -- A
recent lengthy e-mail
correspondence reminded me
of how it was once not

uncommon for me to write
such letters, and the
delight of doing so. It
also made me question the

way I currently interact
with people in the digital
world, something that's
already been on my mind as

I recalibrate my priorities
in life. -- Over the past
few months, I've removed

most   "unnecessary"   apps

from my devices. I stopped
idling on Google Chat, AIM,
and   IRC—the   latter   two
being   services   I'd   used

almost daily for 15 years—
and have been refreshing my
inbox less often. A handful
of objectively unnecessary

apps survived the purge
though, including Facebook
and Twitter.   --   In   my
effort   to   decrease   time

spent on social media, I've
found that I use it more
selfishly.   These days I
only open social apps when

I have something to share,
which feels uncomfortably
narcissistic. The immediate
praise that comes in the

form of likes and faves can

tempt even those who don't care for it. -- My ability to live in the moment and

enjoy everyday life is also diminished, since I tend to snap photos and fumble with my phone instead of

enjoying what's at hand. [Link] Nick Bilton's 2012 New Year's Resolution [Link] comes to mind, and

resonates with me now more than ever. I do love taking photos though—I've just come to appreciate that an

unshared photo is a more meaningful one. -- Don't get me wrong—I prefer to stay in touch with friends

and keep apprised of their lives. But I miss the richness that our interactions once had, and

would much rather catch up
with someone face-to-face
or at least through a true
correspondence, rather than

peek at their life through
the   distorted lens   of
social media posts. -- The
time   and energy I spend

streaming   disjointed
snippets of consciousness
to   social   media   would
undoubtedly be better spent

writing and sharing more
cohesive written works. And
there are better, private
platforms for journaling,

which is primarily what I
use social media for. -- So
today   my   Facebook   and
Twitter   apps   join   the

purge, replaced by trusty
pencil and notebook paper.

If you notice me less on
social media (as I hope you

will), know that I'm still
around, and eagerly await
and welcome your letters.
Or a bicycle ride, walk in

the park, and even just
reading beside one another—
anything but a tweet. - x -
- Congress has rarely

worked a full week in 37
years // winter in DC --
Japan Volcano Erupts; Hiker
Dead, 40 Hurt //

pyroclastic flow -- Geroge
Clooney Ties the Knot // an
old couple wearing glasses
-- Ex-Con Former US Rep

Dies After Tractor Accident
// old man with grey hair
yells into a microphone --
facebook on a phone -- news

feed most recent -- games I
might like, scrabble, the
candy thing, another
scrabble game, play now?

Ren Liam and Cait Black
like Audible, who are
offering me a free
audiobook download of the

latest Neil Gaiman novel,
Stephen saw Juliana
Huxtable, Cait has
something to say about

baskets, Cameron is in need
of motivation to move body,
Jera Sky has a Ghost
Sighting on google maps,

Cait Black via George
Takei: HAPPINESS IS
SUBMISSION TO GOD-ZILLA,
Omar Yazy quotes from the

Koran, Dave hates living in
Philadelphia (10 people
like this), Ren is out

drinking (1 person liked

this), Philly AIDS Thrift
had their 9th Birthday
Block Party Carnival and
the land shark was there,

Juliet has a joke about
Scott the anorexic, John
Wilder was tagged in
Audrial Wilder's photos,

Russell Pasctore has posted
a photo of a woman smearing
blood into her breasts; she
appears to be inside of a

cave (4 people liked this),
MORE STORIES: Edward Newton
is surprised to find out
that SET A BABYWEARING

WORLD RECORD on 10/15/14 at
the Pennsylvania Convention
Center is in fact "a
thing", Jenny Martin

invites us to Come to

golden tea to see Todd
Killings, Ciara is having a
bad day :((1 person liked

this), Caketrain Jouranl
via Gabrial Richard want me
to find out Which Poet I Am
by taking a quiz via

PLAYBUZZ.COM (3 people like
this), Austin Spence is
going to 50 Shades of
Green; where a squirrel

appears to be drinking a
cocktail -- 43 other people
are also going, Dollar
Shave Club reminds me that

getting a kitten is a BIG
COMMITMENT while shaving is
not, Ahn Saunders wishes
happy bday to her babe,

Stephen Boyer went to some
pretentious looking art
show and 2 people like
this, MORE STORIES: Haden

Reed and Stephen Masso
dressed as Disco storm
trooper realness Gabriel
Ojeda Sague, Joey Mason and

13 others like this,
Russell Pascatore suggests
that perhaps this is what
Husserl does, at bottom, by

demonstrating the
irreducibility of
intentional incompleteness
-- this is illustrated by a

screen shot of a woman
performing fellatio on a
man, with a little black
censor box covering her

lips//his dick and 6 people
like this, Dave Garrett
Sarrafian has posted a
picture of McDonalds french

fry box with chopped
lettuce spilling out of it

(5 people like this), in
response to this post

Daniel Mooney has posted a
video of a cartoon spongue
entitled 2-Salads! the
video is of low quality

(image and sound recorded
directly off of a
television screen), it
begins with a large female

whale telling the cartoon
spongue -- who appears to
be dressed as a kleenex box
with two letter K's

attached to springs bobbing
off of his head -- that he
has an order up; sponge bob
reads the order and reveals

that he's never heard of 2
salads before, realizing
that he doesn't want to end
up like a silly old

squidward, but after
swearing profusley he still
cannot figure out what a
sall-ad is, a bunch of

bubbles act as a cut shot
to the next scene in which
the songue approaches the
large whale with two burger

patties (made of crabs),
the whale is offended and
finds this gross, telling
the spongue to take the ill

prepared meal back to the
kitchen: the buns, the
patties & the condiments
must be removed, the sponge

remarks that will only
leave tomatos and the whale
says "exactly" -- back in
the kitchen the spongue --

define spongue: sponge --
removes the buns, ketchup,
the patties and oh yah it's

happening just tomato and

lettus -- define lettus:
lettuce /'letis/ sound icon
noun -- lettuce and tomato
is definitely the coolest

meal   he   ever   saw
(sarcastically)   and   he
drops   this   new   meal,
despondently,   in   front   of

two young fish who think
they are in the coolest
establishment ever while
the sponge dryly remarks

"here's your salad" - X --
Summer of Monuments -- We
need your help documenting
history.   »   Ernesto

Jaconelli From Wikipedia,
the   free   encyclopedia
Ernesto   Jaconelli   (16
December 1917 - September

1999) was a childhood piano

accordion player during the 1930s. Nationally known as 'The wonder boy

accordionist, with lightning fingers'. Contents 1 Early life 2 Musical Success 3 Later

life 4 Television 5 Discography 6 External links Early life Born in Townhead, Glasgow to

Italian parents-Ricc -- Log In -- Hot Topics -- Newser - Current News - Breaking Stories -- home VIDEO

POLITICS MONEY HEALTH TECH US WORLD GREAT FINDS OPINION SCIENCE CELEBRITY ENTERTAINMENT SUPERLATIVES

MORE THE GRID POPULAR -- Set your default tab » -- All Today Yesterday -- Pick a Date -- Mystery "Franken-

Wheat" Crop Appears in
Montana // wheat in a field
-- Man Who Raised $55K for
Potato Salad Throws Big

Party // a man's face
surrounded by potatos --
Elderly "Nice Guy" Shot 4
Times Answering Door //

POLICE LINE DO NOT CROSS --
CEO "Shamed" by Daughter
Into Quitting $100M Job //
man in a suit -- Judge

Rules on Man Paralyzed for
Cavity Search // man in
hand cuffs -- 7 Celebs Who
Got Regrettable Tattoos //

two people who might be
famous? -- Scientists Slip
Bob Dylan Quotes Into
Papers // old bob dylan at

a microphone -- Obama: Yes,
We Underestimated ISIS //

Obama looks calm/composed -
- Kid, 11, Among 15 Shot in

Miami Nightclub -- Here's
the State Whose Drivers Are
the Rudest -- Chris Pratt
"Sharp" as SNL Turns 40 --

Sorry, US: Europe Keeps
Ryder Cup -- Plants in
"World's Most Dangerous
Garden" Can Kill You --

Hong Kong Cops Lob Tear Gas
at "Occupy" Protest --
Ancient "Lost City" Brought
to Life With Lasers --

Elderly 'Nice Guy' Shot 4
Times Answering Door -- 72-
year-old Utah man had no
enemies, neighbor says --

By Neal Colgrass, Newser
Staff -- Posted Sep 28,
2014 3:41 PM CDT -- STORY
// COMMENTS (19) -- Embed

this story -- (Newser) - An elderly Utah man described as "too nice of a guy" answered a knock at his

door last night and was shot four times by an unknown assailant, KSL.com reports. His wife

apparently saw the dark-clothed gunman running away when she hurried to her 72-

year-old husband lying in the doorway. He took four shots to the chest, neck, and head, a neighbor says,

and is still hospitalized in critical condition. "I just don't understand," says the neighbor, Erin

Wyttenbach. "He was too nice of a guy." Wyttenbach adds that he had rental properties, "taking care of

people and all of that kind
of stuff," and she had
"never seen him with any
enemies." --   "On the

surface, it's pretty
frightening," says a police
lieutenant in West Valley
City. "We really don't have

a motive. We're not sure if
it was mistaken identity."
The couple had just
returned from a symphony

concert at 10:40pm when the
knock came, leading
Wyttenbach to believe that
"either they were waiting

for him or they followed
him home or something, I
have no idea."
Investigators tell the Salt

Lake Tribune that no one
has come forth with another

description   of   the
assailant   or   a   possible

motive.   "It's   really
baffling,"   says   the
lieutenant. -- 2% HILARIOUS
-- 1% INTRIGUING   -- 23%

DEPRESSING -- 1% BRILLIANT
--   69%   SCARY   --   3%
RIDICULOUS -- At Least 31

Hikers Presumed Dead Near
Peak of Japanese Volcano --
4 Dayna Evans and 53 others
-- Mount Ontake, a volcano

that spontaneously erupted
in Japan on Saturday, has
left   dozens   of   hikers
presumed   dead   near   its

peak, a spokesperson for
the Japanese police said.
The mountain continues to
spew   dangerous   smoke,

making   rescue   efforts

difficult. » Today 2:40pm --
- Japanese Hiker Captures
Terrifying Video of Mount

Ontake's Eruption --
Kristen Wiig and Bill Hader
Mock Newscaster Who Didn't
See Their Film -- 13 --

Kelly Conaboy and 46 others
-- Kristen Wiig and Bill
Hader are making the promo
rounds for their new film

The Skeleton Twins, which
recently brought them in
front of Denver
entertainment reporter

Chris Parente. Though he
gave it his best shot, poor
old Parente just could not

pull off pretending he'd
actually seen the movie. »
Today 1:32pm -- The

Skeleton Twins and the

Crafting of a Modern Gay
Character -- CNN Guest
Commits Ultimate Fashion

Goof, Wears Same Outfit As
Host -- 4 Dayna Evans and
45 others -- On Sunday
morning's edition of Brian

Stelter's Reliable Sources,
Stelter's guest Jim Miller,
who had come on the show to
discuss the ongoing saga of

Bill Simmons' suspension,
was instead the focus of a
hilarious fashion faux pas.
Stelter and Miller were

dressed like twins. » Today
1:05pm -- fried tofu and --
How To Make Crispy Tofu
Without   Deep-Frying —

Cooking ... -- fried tofu
and from www.thekitchn.com-
-www.thekitchn.com/how-t...
-- Apartment Therapy's The

Kitchn 449 cal -- Mar 17,
2014 - Most foods are made
exponentially more tasty
once deep-fried (witness:

state fair food), but I
feel that this is
especially true for tofu. A
crispy coat ... -- Veggie

Tofu Stir Fry | Minimalist
Baker Recipes -- fried tofu
and from
minimalistbaker.com --

minimalistbaker.com/tofu-
that-tastes-good-stir-fry/
-- Rating: 4.5 - 22 reviews
- 1 hr - 371 cal -- Veggie

and tofu stir fry made
tasty with a special, easy
technique for giving the
tofu more texture and

flavor. Serve over rice or
on its own - a healthy and

... -- mustard and veggies
and I honestly couldn't

finish it. And when it
comes to food I'm a trooper
-- The best part? It wasn't
wet or soft or soggy or

lacking in flavor at all
like all of the tofu I'd
tried prior. She rattled
off a few instructions and

I made a mental note. That
same week I hopped in the
kitchen and gave it a go
mys -- I hope to

incorporate it into more of
the meals we regularly
prepare to see just how
versatile it is. But from

what I've tasted so far, I
have very high hopes. For
the Sauce -- 1/4 cup low-
sodium soy sauce (make sure

it's gluten free if G-Free)
-- 1 Tbsp fresh grated
ginger -- 2 Tbsp brown
sugar -- 1 Tbsp agave,

maple syrup (or honey if
not vegan) -- 1 Tbsp corn
starch -- Easy Vegan Fried
Tofu Recipe - Vegetarian

Food - About.com --
vegetarian.about.com › ...
› Vegetarian and Vegan
Chinese Food Recipes --

Fried Tofu is great on it's
own or dipped in just about
any kind of sauce. You can
also use fried tofu in a

vegetable stir-fry or
noodle dish -- Ingredients
-- 1 block firm or extra
firm tofu -- 3 tbsp

nutritional yeast -- 2 tbsp
flour -- 2 tsp garlic
powder -- 1/2 tsp salt --

1/2 tsp pepper -- 2 tbsp

original recipe. -- for the
peanut sauce: -- 3 tbsp
smooth peanut butter -- 1
tbsp apple cider vinegar or

rice vinegar -- ½ to 1 tbsp
organic cane sugar or as
required - depends upon the
sweetness of the peanut

sauce -- ½ tsp red chilli
powder or red chili flakes
-- ¼ tsp soy sauce -- salt
as required -- preparing

the peanut sauce -- first
combine the vinegar, sugar
and salt in a pan. -- keep
on flame and bring to boil.

tonight with john oliver"
"solarmovie" Episode#1.17
-- the video.me lestr4 L --
play now (thumbs up n/a) --

pop ups -- X -- X -- click

this button to play video -
- this american life -- US
/ CA / AU -- Login /

Register -- Radio Archive -
- Ways to Listen --
Favorites -- Podcast -- TV
Archive -- About Us --

Store -- Donate -- Twitter
-- Facebook -- 536: The
Secret Recordings of Carmen
Segarra -- Sep 26, 2014 --

An unprecedented look
inside one of the most
powerful, secretive
institutions in the

country. The NY Federal
Reserve is supposed to
monitor big banks. But when
Carmen Segarra was hired,

what she witnessed inside
the Fed was so alarming
that she got a tiny
recorder and started

secretly   taping.
ProPublica's print version.
-- play -- Tractors pull
artillery through Kim Il

Sung Square during a
military parade to mark the
65th anniversary of the
country's founding in

Pyongyang, North Korea --
Weibo, China's version of
Twitter, went crazy this
week with reports that Jo

Myong Rok, a North Korean
vice marshal who died four
years ago, had overthrown
Kim in a coup and sent his

lieutenants to South Korea
for negotiations. Talk
spread so quickly that the
Global Times, one of

China's official papers,
ran a commentary Monday

titled "For those who make
up rumors of coup in North

Korea, is it so funny?" --
Sally190 -- He needs a chat
with George Osborne, who
has adjusted his diet to

lose two stones. -- A woman
walks by a pandal art
installation entitled 'Mars
Mission' with the figure of

an astronaut during the
Durga Puja festival in
Calcutta, India -- "we
were" -- Search tools --

Anytime --->the past hour -
- we were pretty starstruck
as well -- we were each
raised in families that

provided us with siblings -
- we were an ok forum -- We
Were Only Aiming for Gold
Medal -- we were young mp3

downloads -- we were going
to the park -- we were most
impressed   with   the
Incredible show events --

See 15325 traveller reviews
-- we were wolves and
Turbogeist   --   "We   were
thrilled to see what he

accomplished. -- we were
just names on a computer
screen -- In response to a
complaint we received under

the US Digital Millennium
Copyright Act, we have
removed 1 result(s) from
this page. If you wish, you

may read the DMCA complaint
that caused the removal(s)
at ChillingEffects.org. --
It's blurry because we were

far -- Who We Are Is Who We
Were -- I knew we were
young and we were gonna be

tested -- we were ready

(against Amarillo), but we
just came out dead --
Reviews for If We Were
Children | FanFiction --

"We were happy with our
performance and where we
are right now. -- Here's to
the good'ole days, before

we were -- before we were
bleeding out of our eyes --
We were just wondering...
From the information on

this page, are you
confident you can tell
which jobs are relevant? --
we were instantly swarmed

with children who awaited
us with pens, paper, and
eager faces -- we were
being taken across the sea

to faraway lands. -- "We

were   ready   to   play
tonight." -- "We were down
by a lot and found a way to

chip back at it. -- we were
able   to   meet   with   the
transplant   doctor,   Dr.
Krance. -- We were skating

a lot in Connecticut, but
you come and skate with a
pro   team,   it's   a   lot
different than skating with

a junior team -- we were
outplayed pretty much every
game until near the end --
We were there from the 22-

26. It rained just about
everyday, but we were able
to make the best of it. --
we were not sure if we

would actually be able to
deliver water -- We were
upgraded straight away when
the staff found out -- We

were just doing the things
that I like, we were
moving, we were moving
without the puck, we were

controlling the tempo, we
were controlling the walls
-- we were not accurate in
our passing and when we

lost too many balls we did
not have enough midfielders
to recover -- We were just
so hyped -- We were storing

your passwords in clear-
text -- "clear text" --
When I asked for
clarification between the

clear text of the state
statute and his words
regarding 'exceeding some
community standard' he said

the 'case law' -- But it
certainly is hair-raising,

and has been cited as part
of the argument for "the

death of clear text" – i.e.
the encryption of all
Internet communications,
including   --   Capture

credentials from clear-text
protocols;   Scan   for
vulnerable hosts on the
network (via PVS); Display

a graph of protocols usage.
-- monitors offer crisp
picture quality, clear
text, and rich colors for

both   home   office   and
business applications.   --
hey are not held in clear
text on any web site.   --

clear -- Cleartext is often
used   as   a   synonym   --
Cleartext is transmitted or
stored text that has not

been subjected to
encryption and is not meant
to be encrypted --
cleartext means including

related links, information,
and terms -- clear text
also displays an extensive
list of geolocation

tracking points (latitude,
longitude), a treasure
trove of security and
privacy -- clear text. Only

if they want to communicate
in clear text over short --
Clear Text Password Risk
Assessment Documentation.

The risks of sending clear
text passwords -- Clear
text password during input:
This problem occurs when

end users type passwords
and those passwords remain
visible on the screen after

being typed -- "after being

typed" -- Search tools --
Anytime ---> Past month --
After being typed, it was
shown to Achdut Ha'avoda

stalwart Israel Gallili and
possibly others, who made
corrections, addendums and
substitutions -- sometimes

with characters appearing a
full 1-2 seconds after
being typed -- After being
typed, it was shown to

Mapai stalwart Israel
Gallili and possibly
others, who made
corrections, addendums and

substitutions, but all in
handwriting -- tenth of a
second: this is time that
it should take for a

character to appear on the

screen after being typed,
for a checkbox to become
selected, or for a short --

how a character gets to the
screen after being typed.
... Distances are measured
in points -- The diary

after being typed up at the
home of Jan -- In order to
show you the most relevant
results, we have omitted

some entries very similar
to the already displayed.
If you like, you can repeat
the search with the omitted

results included. -- water
is not a human right --
product of capitalism in
scrafice zone -- solarmovie

the simpsons -- Watch
Simpsons TV Shows (70 TV
Shows total) - SolarMovie -
- The Simpsons 1989 -- a

grey bubble -- IMDB 8 --
0096697 -- The satiric
adventures of a working-
class family in the misfit

city of Springfield... --
Separate   Vocations   /
Episode 18 -- The Simpsons
-- Season 3 -- Episode 13 -

- 0701204 -- The results of
a standardized test steer
Bart in the direction of
law   and   order   at

Springfield   Elementary
School.   However,   Lisa
becomes so depressed by her
results that she turns to

juvenile delinquency.. --
thevideo.me -- megashowz L
-- POP UP -- ADULT VIDEO
GAME -- X -- PLAY -- Dragon

Flight -- X -- define evoke
-- About 3,050,000 results

(0.18 seconds) -- Search
Results -- e·voke -- i'vōk/

sound icon -- verb -- 1.
ring or recall to the
conscious mind. -- "the
sight of American asters

evokes pleasant memories of
childhood" -- search tools
-- anytime ---> past hour -
- It evokes escapism and

the desire to discover the
inaccessible,   the
undiscovered -- Evoke HR
Solutions -- defines and

assesses completeness of
work Projects Planning
Drives mid-level planning -
- bility to define. ....

Marketing Manager · Evokes
HR Solutions -- Interior
Define,   interlude,
international city event,

international space station
-- North Korea, already
under U.N. sanctions,
prepares launch -- Tesla

Will Announce Something
Called "The D" On October -
- USE OF IBID. -- If two or
more references to the same

work follow one another
without a reference to a
different source between
them, even if separated by

several pages, use "ibid."
rather than the usual
author and title subsequent
notes system. -- Here's an

example. Consider this your
first citation: -- 1.
Patricia Duane Beaver,
Rural Community in the

Appalachian South
(Lexington, KY: University
Press of Kentucky, 1986),

77. -- If the next

reference in your notes is also from Beaver's Rural Community in the Appalachian South, and from

the same page as your previous note, then your very next note would look like this: -- 2. Ibid. --

This means that footnote #2 is from same source and same page as footnotes #1. -- If the next note is also

from Beaver's Rural Community in the Appalachian South, from a different page, then the

next note would look like this: -- 3. Ibid., 65. -- Husband and wife William and Ellen Craft's break

from slavery in 1848 was

perhaps the most
extraordinary in American
history. Numerous newspaper

reports in the United
States and abroad told of
how the two--fair-skinned
Ellen disguised as a white

slave master -- puritans as
fugitives "non-citizens" --
"laws against puritans" --
Arbitrary or oppressive

exercise of power; unjustly
severe use of one's
authority; despotic
treatment or influence;

harsh, severe, or
unmerciful action; with a
and pl., an instance of
this, a tyrannical act or

proceeding -- had entered a
Paradise": Fugitive Slave
Narratives and Cross-Border
Literary History Nancy Kang

is a doctoral candidate at
the University of Toronto,
Department of English. She
specializes   in   African

American literature of the
nineteenth   and   twentieth
centuries, as well as the
poli-   tics   of

interracialism   in   con-
temporary American writing
-- Starting Places: EBSCO
MegaFILE | JSTOR | Web of

Science | Scopus | Google
Scholar All Databases &
Article Indexes: Subject |
Name (A-Z) For all journal

holdings,   see
PennPennTextText   Article
Finder or Franklin E-
Journals: Subject | Title

(A-Z) Subjects/Collections
| Research Guides -- What

kinds of "practice" create
possibilities for new

feminist futures? How do
our everyday engagements
with power complicate how
we understand feminist

struggle? Tina Campt uses
black-feminist concepts to
challenge the notion that
resistance is the only way

to understand the interplay
between marginalized
subjects and power.
Focusing on archival

photographs of black
communities in diaspora,
she explores the daily
practices of black subjects

whose struggles are often
overlooked in an emphasis
on collective and
individual acts of

resistance. The concept of
"fugitivity"   or   "taking
flight" emerges   as   a
signature idiom of black

diasporic culture. This can
be a meaningful pathway for
realizing   the   futures
articulated   by   black

feminist theory. Tina Campt
is   Ann   Whitney   Olin
professor of Africana and
Women's   Gender   and

Sexuality   Studies,   and
newly appointed co-director
of the Barnard Center for
Research on Women. She is

the   author   of   Other
Germans: Black Germans and
the   Politics   of   Race,
Gender and Memory in the

Third   Reich   and   Image
Matters: Archive,
Photography and the African

Diaspora in Europe -- - An

entire amount of felony
convictions, combined to
add character to a
fugitive's actions --

Philadelphia, PA - From
your Internet address - Use
precise location
 - Learn more

This text represents a transcription of the author's use of the internet on one machine during the week of September 25th – October 2nd, 2014. Each "--" represents a shift in attention, each "x" represents the closing of a window, and text that was originally hyperlinked is surrounded by the [LINK] tag. The text is 62 pages long, contains 6,138 words, 28,334 characters without spaces, and 35,123 characters with spaces. All of these numbers are evenly divisible by 3.1. For an interactive web version of this document, please visit: http://windows31.altervista.org/windows3point1.html

www.ingramcontent.com/pod-product-compliance
Lightning Source LLC
Chambersburg PA
CBHW051214050326
40689CB00008B/1306